Pruning Burning Bushes

Pruning Burning Bushes

Poems by Sarah M. Wells

WIPF & STOCK · Eugene, Oregon

PRUNING BURNING BUSHES

Copyright © 2012 Sarah M. Wells. All rights reserved. Except for brief quotations in critical publications or reviews, no part of this book may be reproduced in any manner without prior written permission from the publisher. Write: Permissions, Wipf & Stock, 199 W. 8th Ave., Eugene, OR 97401.

Wipf & Stock
An Imprint of Wipf and Stock Publishers
199 W. 8th Ave., Suite 3
Eugene, OR 97401
www.wipfandstock.com

ISBN 13: 978-1-62032-330-4

Manufactured in the U.S.A.

for Brandon

and for Lydia, Elvis, and Henry

"Nothing is yet in its true form."

—C.S. Lewis, *Till We Have Faces*

Contents

Acknowledgments | ix
Cascade Valley | xi

I. Excavating | 1

Angry | 3
Climbing the American Metal Playground Slide | 4
Ohio | 5
The Pigs | 7
Instructions for the Excavator | 9
Junction | 10
Consider the Sparrows | 11
Sifted As Wheat | 12
Jesus Walks into a Bar | 13
Predator | 14
Levi, After the City of Shechem | 16
Riding After Winter | 18
Honky-Tonk Bride | 19

II. The Need to Be Filled | 21

Harvesting Raspberries | 23
The Bottom Dwellers | 24
Making the Bed | 25
Traveler | 27
D&C (Now I Lay Me Down to Sleep) | 28
Assailants | 29
My Baby Sister | 30
The Milking Room | 31
Thunder | 33

Rain Dance | 34
Measuring Rings | 35
Pruning Burning Bushes | 36

III. Driftwood | 37

Dent de Lion | 39
Crater | 40
Driftwood | 41
Singing Birds | 42
Last Born | 43
Ten Reasons Why He Didn't Die | 44
Aware | 47
Grandfather Dying | 48
Expiration Date | 49
The Japanese Maple | 51
The Antique Rocking Chair | 52

IV. Sunday Worship | 55

Daylily | 57
Sunday Worship | 58
A Christmas Poem | 60
Pancakes | 62
Hymn of Skin | 64
In the violent center | 66
Woven and Spun | 68
Union | 69
Casa Blanca Lily | 70
The ladies' quilting club is out today, | 71
My Mother's Kitchen | 72
Interference | 73

Creek Walk | 75

Acknowledgments

Grateful acknowledgment to the following journals where these poems, sometimes in earlier versions, first appeared:

Alimentum, "My Mother's Kitchen"
Ascent, "Cascade Valley"
Christianity & Literature, "Dent de Lion" and "A Christmas Poem"
Journal of the American Medical Association (JAMA), "Hymn of Skin"
Literary Mama, "The ladies' quilting club is out today,"
Measure: A Review of Formal Poetry, "Sifted As Wheat"
The New Formalist, "Singing Birds"
New Ohio Review, "Making the Bed"
Nimrod: International Journal of Prose and Poetry, "Interference" and "Rain Dance"
Poetry East, "Casa Blanca Lily"
Poetry for the Masses, "Junction"
r.kv.r.y, "Daylily"
Relief: A Christian Literary Expression, "Pruning Burning Bushes"
Rock & Sling, "Honky-Tonk Bride"
The Table (Ashland Theological Seminary newsletter), "Thunder"
Windhover: A Journal of Christian Literature, "Angry"

"Angry," previously titled, "The Angry Gardener," received honorable mention in the Akron Art Museum's New Words 2009 Poetry Contest.

Several poems included in this manuscript were originally published in a limited-edition chapbook, *Acquiesce*, published by Finishing Line Press in March, 2009.

Cascade Valley

Look, my daughter, the pine tree
dropped its seeds, and here
a fragile sapling braves the forest floor.
This used to be a birch tree
but lightning sliced it, wind heaved
its heavy breath and now
the trunk is rust. Sticks once flared
skirts of springtime buds,
but now we throw the broken limbs
into rushing floodwaters
to see how quickly we could be carried
away. Always a hair too close
to the edge, pebbles skitter
into the river. Let's find our way
back from this spring rage, out of the valley
that catches what used to cling
above. Climb this mountain
with its tread marks, hoof prints,
decomposing oaks—we are not the first
to grow and fall. But see the way
the leaves return to earth, the way the dust
collects? Crocus blades emerge
from crumbling stumps as if this growth
does not take more than soil,
light, and rain. Reach down, my child,
bring a pine cone home to show
how miraculously we are carried.

I. Excavating

Angry

> *"He cuts off every branch in me
> that bears no fruit..."*
> —John 15:2

The angry gardener sees
overgrown, untended beds
and seethes. He pulls
the waist-high weeds,
heavy in seed, and heaves
them to the compost heap.

And then the shrubs—
how they shudder
in his shadow, hand saw
pushed and pulled until
limbs quiver, surrender.

Pruners snip, his grip
is sweaty, tight, a frenzy
to the suckers, rose hips,
broken stems, spotted leaves.
The clipping never ends;
he is severe—takes away
more than one-third.

And then mulch,
fertilizer, buckets of water.
The landscape sighs,
breathes with the gardener
who stands back,
fists on hips.

Climbing the American Metal Playground Slide

I am the groove in the "R" at the center
rolling forward, narrative ornate
because I have repainted my primer
of private history emerald green,
replacing the rust-red grit I inherited. . .
though it might only be rouge,
a ruse of erudition over ignorance,
making rubies from the affairs
of faith and farms. I trace the space
between the dirt and my fingertips anyway,
as if to lift the elements of my ribs
from their fissures, a superficial rinse,
surface shimmer. The root of my fruit
is still bruised at the base of the tree.
This rhetoric of theology follows me, I am
swallowed in iambs of nursery rhymes
and grace, grandmother of forgiveness
who handed me the caramel-coated apple
and said *eat all the way to the seed*.
The remaining core is this verse I climb,
every rung branching back
to our revolutionaries. This earth
is ours, its harvest, its rot. This ladder
has our dirt tucked between the crevices
of every letter. I reach and reach,
polish whatever skin I can and trip
over the broken treads, all repeat
American, American, American,
until I reach the peak and slide, hot metal burning.

Ohio

I. Against the Ground

I was wheat-field flat and growing
into rolling foothills. Somewhere in me
were illuminated cities waiting for dawn,
but my factory towns slipped into dusk,
their single-panes broken against mid-day light.

I did not see myself deciduous,
shedding cherry blossoms like wilted promises.
The spruce with its blush of blue growth
led me to believe I was evergreen, but even that
cannot withstand six months of winter salt, of ash.

Snow melts before it hits the earth
as rain in a season I pretend is spring
because the crocus and daffodil return
and the factories churn out shopping marts
and parking lots filled with rusted pick-up trucks.

I wait, perched on my steel I-beam,
for the college students to come home,
but it is spring, and the frost returns to kill the buds
before they've bloomed. The Earth turns,
pushes fieldstones into my hands for harvest

before the plow restores the hollowed stalks
of last year's crop into the dirt. Earthworms
labor alongside the farmer who toils
against the ground, ready for the slow shiver
of crops, slow billow of hope.

II. Soup of the Day

I only knew the many ways to cook
zucchini because there was so much of it
                         and I was tired
of fried, tired of bread, tired of grilled.
I do not sauté; I sauce, I boil, I butter and boy,
                         my boys grow tall.
But now I am old. Unyielding. I do not produce
as much food as I used to. My fields are named
                         suburban neighborhoods.
I eat the meat of other states and export
grain-fed college kids. I do not know
                         how to behave
in this marketplace, how to diversify my menu,
integrate new ingredients. Entrees remain the same.
                         I do not change.

III. Histories

I hold my histories
                 like apologies,
named the river Cuyahoga and walk
          a crooked path past Flats
of abandoned restaurants, wander
          Geauga County trapping
                   the raccoon here

and releasing it there,
               out of sight,
trace the large creek that meanders
         the southern border, utter *Ohio*
and do not know or remember
             the Seneca Indians
would not have added "river"
               to the end, just Ohio.

The Pigs

Dad revived the barn—its siding stripped
for a neighbor's cabinets, the grooved tin roof
rattling in wind on top of rotten trusses—
he buried sagging basement cow stalls
with Midwestern clay and silt, poured cement.
A makeshift pen and pump raised up

our three weaned piglets. I flung half-eaten cobs
in their feeder, rubbed wet snouts,
scratched behind ears, pet stubbled backs.
They rooted, trotted, rolled, and pissed.
We named them Buster, Pinky, Red, and watched
with rested arms on rails for hours.

They escaped one day—split the hillside,
squealed and darted through the valley—
freedom wild in frantic hooves.
I chased Buster with a stick, the dog leash
in my hand dragging through new top soil
in the cul-de-sac. He left prints in bluegrass,

clicked across asphalt driveways and startled
Labradors on porches with his sunburned skin,
until I caught him, walked him home
past landscaped beds. We corralled the hogs
into a truck backed up to the barn on Labor Day.
The concrete floor is clean, a water pump

drips and rusts. The barn cat slinks between
some soggy bales of straw. Look through the gaps

in slats Dad hung. A harvester shredded
cornstalks here, silage suspended in the air.
The sun hung long and bright above the trees
all evening, shadows cast for deer to wander

undetected through rows, acres of long, unending rows.

Instructions for the Excavator

for my father

When you bury a horse
for a neighbor, bring the backhoe
over, dig a trench, tip her in—
the daughter crying by her mother—
when you find her stiff in her stall,
you will have to break her legs
so she will fit.

*

When you dig a basement
ten feet deep, push away topsoil
to reach into clay and scrape
the scoop across a boulder.
Send your brother in to measure;
aim the laser, read a quarter-inch
too shallow. Pound the stone,
over and over—buckets are strong,
excavator's arms won't fracture—
pound the stone, and wait for it
to crack.

Junction

There is no el train in Auburn, no steady rumble
like thunder on a summer afternoon. Suburbans
honk and veer behind my neighbor's combine,

pass, speed up to the light, line up at four-ways
for permission to turn. The Cleveland and Eastern
Interurban used to pass through here,

the Maple Leaf Route curved slow through Newbury
to Amish country, carrying produce and passengers
in to the big city to see a show at the Hippodrome.

Today, the maples shiver along the upraised curve
as if a train has just passed through, but it is only me
or the wind. I do not hear the click-clack on the raised track,

the crowd of travelers standing in the woods waiting
for the junction's switch to take them north or further west.
Now the forest and road are silent; last season's leaves

crunch beneath my feet. Syrup drips from its spile
into cold, steel buckets. A car swings south down
Munn Road, wondering at the slope in the woods

and then the thought is gone. The sun rolls steady on its track
across the blue, though I'm the one who's moving—I
and the farmer and the Suburban and the earth composting

beneath my feet, faster than these fleeting minutes.
How slow the shift in shadows. How soon
I'm surprised to be chilled in the late afternoon.

Consider the Sparrows

> *"Are not two sparrows sold for a penny?*
> *Yet not one of them will fall to the ground*
> *apart from your Father."*
> —Matthew 10:29

So many come, Dad hides behind a blind
with birdshot and a rifle in the grain field.
They scatter, land, scatter, land. I hear them
chirping through the boom, watch their flight
ripple like cotton sheets lifted in the wind.

A sparrow's egg on concrete—the yolk
seeping through the fracture—makes me stop
to look from broken shell to fretting maple
branches above, for the mother who chirrups
in her nest, twitching, head tilted, eyes blinking.

Small sparrow, tomorrow I will walk
beneath your bed just like today,
the ruined egg in smaller fragments, or vanished,
and you will scavenge the earth, fly overhead,
the sky heavy with you and your flock

who will not know me from any other creature
below. I will regard you as just another
house sparrow, attacker who captures
bluebirds in their nestbox,
descends on golden fields of grain.

Sifted As Wheat

> "Simon, Simon, Satan has asked to sift you as wheat.
> But I have prayed for you, Simon, that your faith may not fail.
> And when you have turned back, strengthen your brothers."
> —Luke 22:31–32

Beloved one, Satan has asked to break
you as glass, shatter your erected frame.
And I have prayed for faith to lose its same
rough shapes, to change its cast, while Satan makes
a ruins of the monument you formulate.
I have permitted this attack, however crass,
to come. Your colored panes provoke impasse,
refract the blades of light I emanate.
When he is done, your weathered window pane—
its empty casing unconstrained by glass—
will not permit unhindered rays to wane,
no darkening curtain drawn, no shutters clasped.
The casement free, a glow of mystery
illuminates the rooms you've yet to see.

Jesus Walks into a Bar

It is always darker than it should be,
but over the pool table, a halo
of florescent light. My father
docks at the bar with others, hunched,
feet propped on footrests,
haunches resting heavy in the seat.
Through the haze of Winstons
they watch Nascar. A shaft of light

splits the cloud of smoke when the door
swings open, and a man not so unlike
the deckhands lined up at the bar walks in.
Heads turn and nod, slow hands lift
as he orders up a Miller then tromps
to the juke box in mud-caked boots,
punches in his number, and Hank sings
There's a tear in my beer and I'm crying for you dear...

"Rack 'em up," he grunts. My father
and the stranger call corners, waltz around
the felt taking shots and drinking rounds,
shake hands when the eight ball drops.
The chalk-smeared cue idles on the table.
Dad lays five dollars on the bar,
"This one's on me," and they drink—
to peace, to love, to redemption.

The men at the bar tip their caps and turn
to watch the man descend the stairs
before the door closes. "I hope he returns
someday," Dad says, taking up his bottle,
"That guy's all right."

Predator

> "...then let me not let pass
> Occasion which now smiles, behold alone
> The Woman, opportune to all attempts..."
> —*Paradise Lost*, Book 9, Lines 479–481

The Ferris wheel operator glares down the line
of young daughters. He controls their fate—
the length of their ride, how elated their squeals.
It would not take much to push the lever hard,
send the wheel spinning, but that is not the way

to win. He slips his cigarette to the corner of his grin
and lights the Camel, rolls the pack in his red
shirt-sleeve and leans, arms crossed, waiting
for a careless Eve to catch his eye. *This ferris wheel
can take you higher than you've ever been before*,

he says, cigarette wobbling as he talks. Her eyes
avert, shy lips curve. She touches her hair,
remembers how she pinned it, picked the perfect
earrings, bought the boots that made her legs
look five feet long. Even a devil in carnival clothes

can woo away an angel, send her soaring above
the other riders, elevated beyond the caramel apples,
fresh-squeezed lemonade, *Honey you are sweeter than sugar,
brighter than neon lights, higher than angels themselves, a goddess
in a white tank top* he seems to say with his eyes

as she passes. She feels it, too, a sick sweetness
welling on her tongue, full bag of cotton candy
devoured in one sitting and now she's uneasy.

The ride has to slow sometime. When he's done
and her car descends, she's a little paler than when

it began. He smiles, lingers long, then turns his eyes
down the line for the next bride of Christ,
her lamp lit and burning all night.

Levi, After the City of Shechem

> *"And all who went out of the city gate heeded Hamor and his son Shechem;*
> *and every male was circumcised, all who went out of the gate of his city."*
> —Genesis 34:24

We only wanted revenge, at first,
just a little recompense for their injustice.
When we slipped into the city that night,

our blades were sharp, our spirits sure.
We slid between houses, through the market's
empty stalls and dusty alleys. I almost tripped

on an overturned basket, smashed a fig
with my sandal. We were careful, scouted out
the best method for approach, timed our attack

when they would be their weakest. The first
was easy, sprawled upon his mat, alone.
The knife was smooth against his throat.

The men whose wives draped casual arms
across their chests were harder, but
we soon discovered shock foreshadowed grief.

They caressed the dampening chests
and wept. Some wailed, the younger ones,
with babies tucked between their sheets.

Neither of us wanted to silence a child,
but the mothers understood, clasped their hands
over their children's mouths and stared

as we backed away. When we found the palace,
the sound from the city reached us
like hundreds of howling dogs. We paused

at the garden gate. The noise from below
ascended on the wind. If we failed
to enter now, the king would rise

and form an attack. It was time.
We found Shechem in her arms,
Dinah's hair undone, and raged again,

certain of our mission. He stirred awake
before we reached him, but sore
from three days before, he was slow

to reach his sword, slow to call the guards,
who were slouched at their posts already.
That would have been enough for us,

except for Dinah, her hair damp
with his blood, screaming and clawing
at Simeon's face. He nearly took the sword

to her. I hoisted her over my shoulder,
gripping her kicking legs as she sobbed,
pounding her fists against my back.

She should have known this was for her
good. We walked back to camp
and dropped her, a heap of shuddering

bones and hair and skin,
                                and went back in.
A law is a law, agreement or not.
Should he have treated her like a whore?

Riding After Winter

I pedal chip-and-seal side streets,
reach the creek and brake, swing over
the guardrail and feel the crease
of culvert pipe on thighs.
Metal chills, the flavor of winter
still pungent on each curve.

Water trickles under my swinging legs,
carries the morning rain, broken bark.
Another maple has crashed over the path
where I used to hide and seek, the forest
thick, muscular—leaves full and dripping.
Early grass encases broken limbs.

He's resting over there, a puppy, collapsed
five feet away. I see two flies buzz
above his coat, drawn into blank eyes
staring toward the tar and limestone.
He is not old, not dead long. I thought
I saw him breathe.

It is raining again, so I hoist myself up,
travel back, the hill steep, slick, empty.
A skunk, still whole, remains
in the road. Its warning scent
lingers with the aroma of manure
and earth. This must be spring.

Honky-Tonk Bride

Jesus is dancing like no one is watching
his partner. He smiles and twirls a girl
in a satiny top and high heels. The audience
raises their glasses and pitchers. The dance
floor is packed and they're playing
his song, the one on seducing a love
gone wrong. All of the ways he's tried
to romance her,
                        but she turns her head,
ignores his advances and catches other
cowboys' stares. She is sure the world
prefers a man in a Stetson hat instead
of this wild-eyed dancer, shameless
for her. How effortlessly
                            he turns her,
gathers her into himself as if he loves her
wandering, as if he loves her
doubts, would save her from her
handsome predators every Wednesday,
Thursday, Friday, and Saturday night
from this honky-tonk to eternity.

II. The Need to Be Filled

Harvesting Raspberries

I teeter on steep inclines
of ditches to pick raspberries
on barbed bushes, wild
down the lane. Their juice
drips and stains my fingertips.
I clamber for the next bunch,
shout, "Look over here!"
devour the bright red fruit
before others can reach them,
leaving off-white nubs
of fruitless buds and under-ripe
berries for the next one.

It is in the tipping, plump and ripe,
tumbling from my bowl,
the seeds from berries eaten in haste
planted between my teeth,
it is in the rumbling ache,
the slow hike back
from empty bushes
I realize what precious,
fragile fruit was in my hands.

The Bottom Dwellers

Flippers stirred up the sandy bottom
as you whirled, water spraying out your snorkel.
I flutter-kicked and sculled while you floundered.

Your eyes grew wide and, like the fish,
you wished for metamorphosis, double-sighted
camouflage as bottom-dweller, protected,

but larval swimming kept you thrashing
at the surface. I morphed from lady fish
to your clandestine predator—treading water,

slow, steady lunges until you weakened—
then kicked hard, dove beneath the surface for you,
pushed off the shifting floor toward shore.

Our scaly bodies dripped, heaved on the beach.
Eyes shifted sideways on our return to the ship.
Home, now, flippers and goggles dangling in our closet,

we try to swim together, parallel eyes careful
to keep the familiar feel of gritty sand against our bodies,
no matter how many thousands of feet deep we must go.

Making the Bed

I think the sheets are missing our twisting—

I heard them bickering this morning

when I tucked the flat 400 thread-count

Egyptian cotton tight against the fitted,

both impatient with our neatness,

pajamas folded on the hope chest.

Even the box spring exhales

when lights dim, but nothing.

It has been too long and now

we have disappointed the whole house—

you should have seen the way the couch

looked at me last night when I sank

into the cushions with my book.

The furniture, appliances, linen closets know—

every cup in the kitchen has been watching

our side-stepping as we spar over dinner.

Here we sit, evening news ending,

like every other tired couple turning off

the television, rolling over, curtains whispering,

wondering, lingerie sidling with socks,

pillows everywhere sighing into pillowcases.

Traveler

We have conceived you,
        and though I am heavy
with you in my womb,
        no one can see it,
your arms being carved,
        heart beating hard
in its five millimeter seed.
        Oh, child of mine, grow,
grow. I want to keep you,
        but you are unable to be
possessed. I carry you
        in me, traveler
from my right ovary. See the cyst
        you left? This is the first
of the damage you'll leave behind.
        We'll grow and gain together
and then you'll leave,
        maybe tomorrow,
                forty weeks, sixty years.

D&C (Now I Lay Me Down to Sleep)

No, I do not want to feel
the slow passing,
        cramping pain
for days. Remove
the tissue and fluid (now)
while I (lay me down
        to) sleep
a dreamless hour,
wake heavy after,
        medicated,
thirsty and unable to
drink because of nausea,
this involuntary purging.
        (I pray the Lord
my soul to) Keep me
here to rest in this hospital
        bed. (If I die)
Before I wake, I will imagine
pastel blankets, a bassinet.
Then (I pray, oh God),
        the vital monitor,
TV tray, traces of blood
on sheets and (my soul)
        the place I cradled,
the hollow womb
filled with no baby
(to take)
        no more.

Assailants

A pair of bluebirds perch beside the nestingbox.
They keep trying to fly in, twitter as they flutter,
but a sparrow blocks the entrance.
The bluebirds cheep and flap their feathers,
fly frantically to the telephone wire. The male
bird settles near the nestingbox on the roof
and she follows, the female, a mother like me.

They chirrupchirrupchirrup, look at each other
then away, send warning voices down to the bird
whose head looks out from their hole, then fly
to the wire again. This is the dance of catastrophe.
I despise the sparrow, its innocent peep, its spindly legs.
We lost four to dark assailants. I wish the bird
would fly away and let the nestlings be. Those are my eggs.

My Baby Sister

When the baby comes back from heaven
she will need these plastic spoons. Lend her
my polka-dotted dress, ruby slippers—
they will fit, if she comes soon. By then,
I will be tall and (see my fingers?) seven,
big enough to help you dress her, tie her
curls in purple ribbon. If she's a crier,
I will find her pacifier. Where is heaven?

If she has to stay away, then let's go visit.
I can feed her carrots (they're my favorite).
Even though they're baby toys, I'll play
and help her learn new things. Can we stay?
I packed my doll, a bib, a dish, these spoons.
I'm ready, Mommy. Will our ride come soon?

The Milking Room

> *"Let no mother condemn herself to be a common
> or ordinary cow unless she has a real desire to nurse...
> Women have not the stamina they once possessed."*
> —Mrs. Panton, Circa 1860

In the dairy barn, the calf is pulled from the cow,
an udder replaced by latex nipples, glass bottles
filled with powdered buttermilk and whey,
then two pounds of grain, water, Bermuda hay.
The simple suckle of the calf substituted
with stainless steel, rubber-wrapped tubes,
the cow in line like so many other mothers,
waiting her turn in the milking room.

I am a milk machine the first three weeks,
latching a plastic apparatus to my breast and waiting
twenty minutes before switching, hooking up again
two hours later to provide my neonatal breast milk
through a feeding tube. All I do all day is pump
and stare, pump and stare. We learn together
how to eat, how to feed under a blanket
with lactation specialists, husband, nurses
near, waiting for the two of us to fail.

The calf walks from uterus to udder, latches
and feasts his first meal with no coaching.
The cow licks her baby's skin, cleans his slick coat
while he tugs her, thirsty for the first fresh sip
of colostrum. They find each other here:
he discovers the nuzzle of a mother's muzzle
on his rump, the warm wet mouth alarming
and delightful on her udder.

The motorized pump hums and sucks.
I want to feed my son, soothe his shaking hands
and hungry arching back but can't. I defrost
frozen milk in plastic storage bags: measured,
and dated in two hour intervals, August 14, 8 p.m.,
August 14, 10 p.m. I would have propped him up
with a feather pillow and a bottle called "The Killer"
if it were 1860, fed him fresh cow's milk
in a banjo-shaped bottle impossible to clean.
The odds were eight in ten dead before two,
dead before able to ask for food.

I am no common, ordinary cow.

Thunder

A clap that can't be named, an after-effect
of condensation rising, electrons colliding,
a cloud's charged particles frenzy
for harmony, the molecular breakdown
as this bi-polar party ionizes air and then

the split and zag across the sky that sucks
breath from lungs, closes throats. I flinch
at sudden, silent light and wait,
head crouched, feet close together,
seconds counted 'til the air explodes.

In the midst of hydrogen and oxygen
zinging like spirits seeking heaven, fleeing hell,
lightning touches down and leaves its mark
emblazoned in a tree, the kind of wound
it takes to heal. Thunder shouts

in long, rippling rounds across the earth.

Rain Dance

We watched the clouds suck moisture
from the atmosphere like an animal
at a water trough and hurried the children
home to park their bikes. The rain began,
a steady shower and then it sliced across the field
in sheets. Our children danced and shrieked
as the sky's giant sprinkler erupted in a wild riot.
Soon the yard was swallowed in the sound of water
rushing over giddy laughter, pounding
the tin roof awning, gushing down the gutters.
Flowers sighed in the drenching, every muddy stone
echoed the cleansing prattle on their granite.
From underneath the overhang, we witnessed
their marvelous bodies dripping,
ours goose-bumped, dry, fearful
for their wet feet, electric souls. What changed
that made us stay behind the door,
what kept us from going out into the storm
with head tipped back, mouth open, our spirits
reckless with praise and the need to be filled?

Measuring Rings

Settle your shifting vision on the maple stump
your son is standing on, growing out
of all your ancient history. The past keeps repeating

in new rings, health you measure by breadth.
You count the number of times you've grown
out of the fire, layers of heartwood healing

over scars, new branches jutting from woundwood.
Stop searching for ways to hollow out your trunk.
It is hard to distinguish redemption from regret;

you must see heartwood for what it is—dormant,
but solid—here only so you have something
to grow on, matter to attach your sapwood.

If the sun will rise to warm your town, you'll take
this trail tomorrow, but it will never be the same—
you cannot pilfer this moment in your pocket

to pull out a year from now. Without your toddler
bouncing on the stump, there is no coaxing down,
no upward-reaching hand, no march on the sidewalk.

Every dead and living branch you've wished away
would erase this knot, this casual miracle
sprouting light with every hallowed breath.

Pruning Burning Bushes

I am over-pruning burning bushes
that border my front porch on Morgan,
cutting back two-thirds of growth
to trigger recovery from the trunk up.
Horticulturalists wince as I saw
through oldest limbs and keep going—
the shrubs are ancient, nothing new is budding.

Someone buzzed them back before we bought
the house, topped and tipped instead of using
crown reduction. There are a dozen leaves left,
tiny offshoots triggered—bursts of green
from long dead, empty stems. My trimming

is traumatic. The branches bend, sustained
so long by suckers sprouted in haste. Here I am,
sighing, sweating, fists on hips, pruners
lost in the grass. The landscape breathes.
There is no exchange, no return in trauma—
either slowly hollow, heartwood rotting outward,
or grow from green into a fiery blaze in autumn.

I pick the pruners off the earth, dust
my aching hands and look for where
the calluses will form.

III. Driftwood

Dent de Lion

I have let loose so many—picking
every bulbous stem to bleed the milky sap—
my palms stick together, seeds crushed
between fingertips. I rinse away
beginnings in the catch basin

filled with summer rain. What are prayers
but dandelions whose fragile seeds
parachute throughout the field behind our home,
carried by my shallow breath to settle
indistinct for the rest of this season.

Even now, I know I will return to the field
with a garden spade next spring
and wonder at the brittle, branching,
ten-inch taproots that took hold,
the way the wind carried those seeds,

how some discovered fertile, merciful earth
and embedded their retorts to my flimsy wishes—
a lion sinking its teeth into his kill.
I split and braid the stalks into a crown—
each head, a hundred golden flowers.

Crater

Wrap your atmosphere around me—
I do not want to be the moon,
unable to deflect the smallest cosmic speck.
I flinch and dodge a thousand bullets
in a meteor shower, yearn to watch
this light show fearless.
Without you, my surface is sensitive—
I bruise at the slightest affront,
scurry away to nurse each hurt.
If I must wear the craters
of implosions and exterior stoning,
dress them in deep blue water
with stunning clarity so none will question
why this happened but know
that nothing so beautiful and pure
could come without pain.
Plant in my volcanic cavity
a hemlock tree so all will witness
how you've rooted yourself
in my explosive fragility
and called me strong.

Driftwood

We are two limbs of tangled driftwood—spin
and stumble through the narrow rivers, twist
in faster currents, drown in driven mists
of falling water. Rocks are closer, lichened
river sandstone, loosened, stumbles free.
How do I not break you, our throes violent,
austere? Commingled boughs are bent—
I could snap in half, take part of you with me.

But water makes us softer—we are blending,
a blur of bark and heartwood, older, harder—
our sharper edges smoothed, severe refining.
Even pebbles once were upstream boulders.
The knotted whorl left over in the widening
estuary rests holy, polished, pure.

Singing Birds

When pairs of chattering birds dart in and out
of trees as if distance will calm the fight,
I hear the parting two prepare
a song, some lonesome twittered sighs.
So when they meet again, the voices rise—
ring true the time they lost by sudden flight.

Lost in bitter sentence fragments, we fall
so far from seeing eye to eye, our words
have silenced every sullen argument.
But wandering eyes and anxious hands may break
the wordless air, and hands composed to shake
entwine in held duet: like singing birds.

Last Born

My final incarnation,
word of hope made flesh
in me—the hour draws
nearer. Right now, you nudge
my ribcage with your hand,
or elbow, or knee. Season
of mystery, I drink
a glass of sweet tea
to feel you move in me. . .
If only joy always came
so easily. For now I am
indwelt, possessed
by holiness, but soon
I will be an open wound,
abandoned, singular but
whole. Every living thing
must grieve as its last seeds
leave, like me, aware
that any blessings after this
will just be birthed on earth,
miracles delivered everywhere,
every ordinary day. No more
my pulse so close to yours.
No more will come
from this womb—it is time
to rejoice, time to mourn.
You are my last born.

Ten Reasons Why He Didn't Die

for Elvis Elijah

The Elvis Lives fan club boasts
ten reasons why he didn't die
seven days after and thirty years
before you were born.
They say he faked it, escaped
under the witness protection plan,
abandoned family in his will
five months before. Breaking news:
he released a new album in 2002.
They spelled his middle name
wrong on his tomb. Graceland
waits for the King to return
to the jungle room.

I walk into the operating room
as if we are only visiting, touring
the facilities for someday weeks away:
this is the table
on which you will be delivered,
there, the sink
where they will wash you,
prep you, hand you back to be held
like you've never been held before.

You who were yet nameless
waited, unaware we were coming
in to get you, breathing
amniotic fluid, blinking
away the red glow:

fluorescent spotlights aimed.
Together, we sit on the table;
I lean over, feel you squirm,
the needle long and in my spine,
cold, numb.

Was it then you knew
or did we sneak up on you,
the surgeon's knife opening
an unexpected exit—startling
as the sudden scream
your sister makes, violent
like the cellar door flung open—
your panicked, shaking jump
a spasm of arms and legs
and gasps as, surfactant-less,
you tried to cry.

Jesus, Moses, Elvis, and Elijah
hover in the waiting room, singing
*I Can't Help Falling in Love
with You*, flipping through
cable but nothing is on
except televangelists
and an announcement
commemorating the 30th year,
the anniversary of Elvis's death.
They are standing with my husband
in blue jumpsuits.

The dark eyes, black hair
I didn't expect and sideburns!
*Are we really going to name him
Elvis*, I ask, running the "el"

over my tongue and hissing the "vis".
Why not Elijah; Elijah sings, rises
out the mouth, ends warmly,
reappears with Jesus.

In your incubator with monitors
and wires, you are intubated,
the over-rhythmic rise and fall
like the hee-haw of a muted
donkey, the see-saw of your name
repeated EL-vis, EL-vis, unlike
any other infant in the nursery.
You are hypnotic and we stare,
asking only for breath, just air
to come and go as if it were natural.

You latch on to a feeding tube,
snuggle with a cloth I've rubbed
my scent into. *Love me tender*
I whisper in the plastic door,
gripping warm, limp fingers,
love me true.

Aware

Before breaking surface, ears pop,
        pressure lightens, there is an absence
of color—captured light in water bubbles
        blending and then air—elements congregating—

I bob like a buoy, anchored by some mysterious
        weight to the floor of the sea but treading water,
aware of the separation of vapors. The ocean
        is erratic as I drift, rolling under, around, above,

lulling by its distant crashing. Close my eyes, body
        released to sink beneath until only upper body lifts,
air resting briefly on my chest and lips before pushed
        away, the ocean rising over. I am above and below.

The dolphin must keep half his brain awake
        to stop from drowning while he sleeps, float
at surface level to inhale, exhale, one eye open,
        watching for a predator other than the sea.

I do not have to remember to breathe.

Grandfather Dying

When you were watching me die,
you with deep faith, your well-meaning prayers
whispered in my ear, I was slowing
my feet from their muffled shuffle
to the front porch. Pap-Pap stood there,
bundled in a gray wool coat and grave
manner. When I saw him,

I started running
in my knickers and polished black shoes, home
from Sunday communion.
My feet carried me easily
over the gravel driveway.

I did not trip
up the steps where my father stared down.
A hand that was not my own
gleaned the sweat from my forehead
Father, bring peace, surrender, release
I wrapped my chubby arms around his legs
and reached.
For once, he lifted me.

Expiration Date

for Rhonda 'Ma'Wells

Mastering the art of preservation,
we hold on beyond the sell-by date,
keep our iceberg lettuce in the crisper.
A day will come when we will need

a bag of shredded zucchini. Of course,
there is the occasional blood-letting
of perishables that withered in our fridge
but appear to be edible a little while longer.

It is an exercise in letting go, opening
our fists and freeing what we cling to.
All the food intends to do is forget
our well-meaning attempts to make it last

and hasten its return to the dust of the earth.

I am tempted to say something about dying here,
about being plugged in to twenty machines.
I want to say I will want you to let go of me
when it is time, even if it is before my time

and technology will preserve my slow descent
into darkness for you, but now I am talking
about my life. What I would decide for me.
Not about you, my husband, whose grip on life

would be hard and steady, even on IVs
and breathing machines. You could not

expire, not now, maybe in four decades
and after I'm gone, but hang on a minute,

don't throw that one away, the expiration
date is just a marketing tactic
to make you buy more salad dressing.

The Japanese Maple

I planted it—a memorial to my father
on the northeast corner of the drive—
so I could see it every day and know
that he is home. It came with a one-year
warranty in case it died. A harder
winter than we've had in years, I waited
through the April rain. Daffodil blades
emerged—I even saw the buds on sugar
maples come. No new canopy burst
from the Japanese maple. Its six foot
stem extended toward the heavens,
naked, brittle. I bent a twig to see
if there was green but, *snap!* it separated
from the tree. I should have found
a shovel, my receipt, returned the empty
branches to the nursery. But today,
I noticed at the base—a six-inch shoot
with minute, maroon leaves. I cannot
separate the living from the dead.

The Antique Rocking Chair

The carpenter is not disappointed
by the ruined finish or the broken arm,
loose spindles, failed glue joints.

He checks the chair for its rhythm,
rests carefully in its solid seat and tests
the sway, hums an ancient hymn,

feels the wind that wore away the finish,
drove the rain between the grains
and diminished the lacquered polish.

A chip along the armrest where a son
discovered mischief with a chisel
can be remedied, the crimson

scribble across the headrest should be
buffered out easily. He takes a pin punch
and hammer, twists the spindles free.

The worn seat board is planed to true
the surface; he's careful to avoid removing
too much wood. And when he's through

clamping cauls, filling end-grain breaks
and feathering maple wedge ends, he
carefully spreads the stripper paste

in heavy coats, waits for the softening
and scrapes away the residue. A putty knife
lifts bubbled layers of tired stain.

Away goes the ache of discoloration,
oil dissolved, original grains exposed.
Every crevice is cleansed, each abrasion

doctored with twine between the grooves,
brass-bristled brushes in each recess.
He sands away the raised grain, removes

the marks in the concave seat. With glue
that's slow to set, the seat and arms are raised
and then the spindles and splat. It's almost new,

the way the old has been removed. The carpenter
knows the chair won't last without stain
and picks a distinguishing shade to bear the wear

of another century. It is set apart, protected
with three coats of clear wood finish. The rocker
holds the woodworker: it is finished.

IV. Sunday Worship

Daylily

I tuck away my secrets
in my tepal until
it is time to trumpet
every petal and sepal,

calyx open, throat laughing.
I may be a common
daylily, but today
I will unfurl, wave

my stamen and declare
myself *Hemerocallis*—
it is mine, this day,
this beautiful day.

Sunday Worship

Heavy dew remains on fronds of corn
in rows I pick at dawn. The leaves of stalks
rustle, stir; we crack away ripe ears
and hear a chorus of thuds in wicker baskets,
eager to fill until too heavy for lifting,
overflowing, tumbling into the lane. My father,
brothers, cousins, aunts, and uncles take
a row, pull away the harvest with a quick twist
of wrist and feel the fragile kernels harbored
safe inside for ripeness, aware of nothing
more than corn, vulnerable and waiting to be taken.

This year is bad. The Platinum Lady—her pearl
white kernels sheltered close to the stalk—
infected with smut, the black fungus a swollen
pustule in the ear, spreading to tassels. We are angry
at deer for dining so shamelessly, leaving half-eaten
cobs attached to the stalk. My aunts whittle
ear worms out of pickings before selling all summer,
pull back tassels to find the caterpillar's
paths grooved, an entire crop ruined.

But this morning, tender white and golden kernels
wait beneath the husks, perched easily
on each stalk. We walk the rows and place
our bushels in the truck. They fill to overflowing,
corn piled high above the bed as we drive, bouncing
down the path to lift each basket, a cloud of dust
behind us. We kneel on the tailgate, the sun above
the tree line warm on our chapped hands and legs,
minutely cut from blades of stalks in the aisles.

The field is empty now; my bushel full
of Sugar & Gold waiting at the end of the row.
How Sweet It Is to feel the vapor of the air
in my clothes, soaked and sticking, absorbing heaven.

A Christmas Poem

I took the fruit
of some body,
mixed it with
the fruit of earth,
birthed harmony
in each small cookie—

Mary's sowing,
reaping, crushing,
sifting, the cow
with milk to give,
hen with eggs to
fold in. This season
announces the melding
of flesh with spirit.
Remember

our miracles blossom from trauma

and this baking is
beating ingredients,
separating
dough in heaping
spoonfuls, elements
indivisible—
egg and sugar,
wheat and water.

Bite in, lick
the crumb
from your upper
lip, partake in this
communion. Now
we are all here:
laborer, consumer,
life-giver, hovering
over the tray.

Pancakes

Grandpa stacked them seven high
with a dab of butter, all-you-can-eat
after a Friday night sleepover.
I cut the circles into even squares, drizzled
maple syrup on each spongy morsel,
soaked up sugar in each pore like memory.
I was ready to flip the cakes before the bubbles
popped—they never cooked fast enough—

but campground pancakes baked quick
and burnt easy over the fire pit. The recipe
for simplicity: add milk, shake and pour
out the weekend hitched to a pick-up truck.
We percolated coffee from rain
off the camper's canopy, burned
all that sucrose on our bicycles
beneath the sugar maples. It turned out

to be a bad idea to help Mom clear the table—
the Aunt Jemima bottle was heavier
than I expected, my grip not sticky enough.
ER doctors removed the sliver of her
glass skirt from my foot. They couldn't read
it in the charts—surprised to see syrup oozing
from the cut—but it was in my genes:

the sugar shack louvered at the roof to vent
the steam. Grandfathers have been boiling sap
for centuries, tapped the maples
and put down their muskets for a short stack.

Pour it from the mason jar—it comes out quicker
than your high fructose corn syrup,
plastic pop-cap brand—this is pure,
thinner; use less—it's sweeter. We follow

the supreme recipe—measure milk and mix,
crack an egg, warm the griddle. This ritual
is a slow rise, tea pot whistle, cooking oil
sizzle—a morning worth a thousand
silver dollars. The rest of the day
may be impatient to begin—summer
whispering through the open window.
Unwilling to wait for vanilla, two tablespoons

of sugar, my daughter stirs the batter
with her wire whisk, *Is it ready yet?* No,
we need more time to spoon the sweetness in.
Dad settles at the table, cup of coffee
and the paper, son stretches to be lifted
to his lap, and we gather, spread the butter,
say grace and pray for grandparents.
Pass the plate of pancakes, please.

Hymn of Skin

Touch this one inch of skin and send
a thousand nerve endings to their knees.
Prick it and risk the run of twenty blood vessels.
Sever this layer to enter the dark territory

of the interior—a six inch scar lets nothing out
that ought to stay in. And how about those
sixty thousand melanocytes per inch that determine
the color of me and when over-exposed to UV rays,

can bring the death of me. This one really gets
under my skin—sweat glands in my palms begin
to kick in. Praise, anyway, to the maker
of the excess folds around my knuckles, ankles,

and knees so I can sit cross-legged and curtsy
with no pain, hold a pen without tears between bones,
metacarpals popping out to be tucked back in.
Glory to the lord of fingerprints, heart lines,

head lines, life lines, indents and cavities
fashioned in the womb. How particular your carvings,
how precise your instrument to etch that patterned
Arch, Whorl, or Loop unique in every instance.

Plastic surgeon of the heavens, how I delight
in a furrowed brow, crow's feet, age spots—
wrinkle me up a dozen times to show I lived
hard, good, funny—after all beauty, being what it is,

is only skin deep—may my soul seep through
dry scales of later hands, resting tranquil in my lap.
O Omniscient dermatologist, what ingenuity,
past hurts evident in scrapes and scars—

a clumsy stumble down uneven concrete stairs,
knees and ankle raw and dripping; pockmarked cheeks
from teenage zits—all healed, in the end, but not forgotten.
How often we need reminders of where we've been.

In the violent center

a cell detonates. Its atomic
cloud slips from zygote
to blastomere, morula to blastocyst.
All of this division is brittle
as bubbles puddling on the edge
of my wand. I wait for the whisper
of air on lips to carry them away.
So many have been duds, broken
before I know any of it. If it is me
responsible for the microscopic
split and growth, then I can see
why the outlines of the air-filled
globes explode on the pavement
at my feet. But what if it is you
who breathes life into these
steady multiplications? Exhale,
please. Only one or two lift off
over the roof. The rest crack,
split, rupture, shatter, fall away.

But one or two lift off
over the roof, drift to the edge
and stick. It clings, all the time
separating into layers and then
it folds, creating the symmetry
I see in me. There are twenty-six
steps to make a paper crane.
I have stopped at figure one
in this organic origami, preparing
to crease the next layer. Here

the paper trembles. Patience,
patience—it will not feel
without its nervous system,
cannot see, smell or hear,
will have no hair or skin—let
the ectoderm have its time.
Stretch the days to make
the visceral and muscle,
elements of the mesoderm
proliferate and migrate.
I breathe again and feel
the work of the endoderm
in those early folds, check
my pulse, digest the ingested
sandwich, listen closely
to the sound reverberating
in my tympanic cavity.

There was a breath.
Did it carry here? I am impulsive,
creative, indulge me in this
dream—are you here now?
Open the body by blowing
into the hole underneath,
then gently pull out the wings.
The paper crane takes flight
and I see a hand stretch out,
but whether yours or mine
remains a mystery. I know
the steps, the creases, which
layers drift, migrate, join.
I could follow the diagram.
But it is not my hand, is it?

Woven and Spun

This strand of life
we've braided
holds enough history to be
a length of DNA.
Tucked between the kisses given
in quickened passing
and longer-lasting glances
is a trust
like hydrogen bonds
between the bases
thymine and adenine
set to stabilize our double spiral.
After all, your helix is mine
and its twisting is witnessed
in these living beings
we've created.
But even when it's just
me and you around,
our chemical reactions
off interacting in this world,
we will stay bound,
double helix woven and spun.
Our bodies seize the space
of atoms, your soul, legs, fingers, eyes
entwined with mine.

Union

for Michael and Hilary

To find a wife more treasured than gems in small
Midwestern towns involves a law of chance
and fate, stars aligned on grocery shelves. Walks
down Brookside paths ensure two souls can dance
as one, the notion now of life alone
as true as Donne: Whatever did we do
                              before?
    Love unfolds in long, slow tones,
formerly unknown but deep and true,
a rhythm grows and blooms from quiet hints
to sudden adoration. Brings a man
to pledge devotion to his wife who glints
with grace, their union one of praise. More than
music, more than man can orchestrate—
holy harmonies will forever resonate.

Casa Blanca Lily

> *"Like a lily among the thorns,*
> *so is my darling among the maidens."*
> —Song of Solomon 2:2

for William and Rachel

I pray you'll have a Casa Blanca lily
love, a strain with fragrant romance keen
enough to tolerate each other's heat,
disease-resistant, strong against the chilly
winter frost. Let your love be giant.
Blossom lavishly so every flower
can see what God has joined together
to grow this oriental hybrid plant.

Surround yourself with strong, embracing
vines who lift you up and give you breath.
Settle among the shrubs whose height and depth
will match your lavish joy, abundant grace.
Bloom in such a way that others strive
to hope, to serve, to love, and thus, survive.

The ladies' quilting club is out today,

their floral dresses, low brown leather heels
and stockings shuffle from a bus
to the restaurant. Sunday hats cover

graying buns, thinning heads. Their coffee cups
clink and shake to painted lips. They make me look
so young, their penciled brows, rouge,

heavy foundation creased. I hold
my daughter's flawless hand past their table,
wait for our turn to collect change at the register.

My Mother's Kitchen

Though I know you
love to rearrange
the furniture to create
a change in scenery,
I am sad to find
the spices where
the dishes used
to be. I want a bowl
to hold some oatmeal,
the same I used
before I moved,
the one I left behind.
The cereal is for my
son, who perches on
the same kitchen
stool where I sat,
listens to the same
radio on the counter,
constant noise
vibrating air as I open
and close the cabinets
again, expecting
this time the stack
of ceramic bowls,
find instead cinnamon,
anise, thyme mixing
savory and sweet
with bitter herbs.

Interference

What right do you have to poeticize
the setting sun, drooping roses,
withered ferns, the urgent marching
of the rising and dying natural world?
Isn't it enough for mourning
doves to raise their young in shifts,
the father slipping in through dew
to relieve the hungry mother?
But every scattered acorn,
every broken limb demands
a stanza, some anthropomorphic
significance. Were these objects made
for your scrutiny—after all, why else
do pin oaks cling to leaves
except to demonstrate the way
you hold on to what has passed,
why else do tulips bloom in May
except to celebrate the end
of this season's darkness with a playful
kiss, betrayal sending death hurling
into spring. Fated poet, pause with pen
suspended, permit the wind its awe,
allow the branches their trembling,
consent the earth its holy inhumanity.

Creek Walk

Wading in the river—current
        pulling me in like
                sliding under covers—
I become part of the riverbed, sediment
        blending with my skin. I am woven
                with wild grasses on banks,
molded to the surface of earth
        in perfect curves, body fluid, rooted.
                I could be washed away with a little rain.
What trickles harmless around me now
        exposes roots of ancient trees
                that lean toward light,
grow sideways to keep from sliding.
        They will join the rapid flow,
                deteriorate with me and we will deposit
in a delta with every other swallowed figure
        from upriver. I dip my fingers in,
                feel the stream make room for me.
I will share in this shifting
        of earth—dirt loosened
                until the roots give way.

www.ingramcontent.com/pod-product-compliance
Lightning Source LLC
Chambersburg PA
CBHW051714090426
42736CB00013B/2704